DELICIOUS DETOX SMOOTHIES

100 EASY-TO-MAKE RECIPES TO HELP YOU DETOX

DARBY WINTRINGHAM

Disclaimer

The information contained in this eBook is meant to serve as a comprehensive collection of strategies that the author of this eBook has done research about. Summaries, strategies, tips and tricks are only recommendation by the author, and reading this eBook will not guarantee that one's results will exactly mirror the author's results. The author of the eBook has made all reasonable effort to provide current and accurate information for the readers of the eBook. The author and its associates will not be held liable for any unintentional error or omissions that may be found. The material in the eBook may include information by third parties. Third party materials comprise of opinions expressed by their owners. As such, the author of the eBook does not assume responsibility or liability for any third party material or opinions. Whether because of the progression of the internet, or the unforeseen changes in company policy and editorial submission guidelines, what is stated as fact at the time of this writing may become outdated or inapplicable later.

TABLE OF CONTENTS

SUPER GREEN SMOOTHIES...................................85

HIGH PROTEIN GREEN SMOOTHIES...............110

DETOX SMOOTHIES FOR BREAKFAST............139

DETOX SMOOTHIES FOR LUNCH.................168

DETOX SMOOTHIES FOR DINNER.................. 197

CONCLUSION.. 222

INTRODUCTION

What is Detox?

Detox is basically the cleansing the intestines as well as the internal organs by a change of diet.

Our bodies naturally detox every day. The body has its own cleaning system that works constantly—by urine, faeces, sweat, and with our breath, we constantly detoxify.

We take in toxins from pollution, chemicals, and food additives, but also by medicine and tobacco. But the worst pollution is self-inflicted by eating junk food or food combinations that are not good for us. The food remains undigested in the intestine, which causes it to putrefy, allowing toxins to spread into the blood stream through the intestinal wall. It encumbers the kidneys and liver, whose job it is to detoxify us and clean out these substances.

When bowels and internal organs become congested, various imbalances occur in the body and you may feel depleted, tired, have sore joints, and suffer from insomnia. In many cases, nutritional therapists recommend first doing a detox before determining a diagnosis, just to make it easier to see what the real problem is.

Why Detox/Cleanse the Body?

When the body is overloaded with toxins, it transfers energy away from burning calories to work harder to detoxify the body. In other words, the body does not have the energy to burn calories.

However, when the body is efficiently getting rid of toxins, the energy can be used to burn fat.

You must first rid your body of toxins to ensure that your body can best metabolize the food you eat without leaving excess waste, which results in weight gain.

Smoothies greatly help with this!

Criteria for a Great Detox Smoothie

A. It needs to look gorgeous: We eat first with our eyes, and nobody wants to drink anything that looks like swamp water!

B. It needs to be mind-blowingly delicious

C. It needs to be nutrient-dense with awesome ingredients.

BEGINNERS CLEANSING SMOOTHIES

1. Berry Green

Ingredients:

- 3 handfuls spinach
- 2 cups water
- 1 apple, cored, quartered
- 1 cup frozen mango
- 1 cup frozen strawberries
- 1 handful frozen or fresh seedless grapes
- 1 stevia packet (add more to sweeten, if necessary)
- 2 tablespoons ground flaxseeds
- OPTIONAL: 1 scoop of protein powder

Directions:

a) Place leafy greens and water into blender and blend until mixture is a green juice-like consistency.

b) Stop blender and add remaining ingredients. Blend until creamy.

2. Apple Strawberry

Ingredients:

- 3 handfuls spring mix greens
- 2 cups water
- 1 banana, peeled
- 2 apples, cored, quartered
- 1 ½ cups frozen strawberries
- 2 stevia packets (add more to sweeten, if necessary)
- 2 tablespoons ground flaxseeds
- OPTIONAL: 1 scoop of protein powder

Directions:

a) Place leafy greens and water into blender and blend until mixture is a green juice-like consistency.

b) Stop blender and add remaining ingredients. Blend until creamy.

3. Apple Berry

Ingredients:

- 1 handful spring mix greens
- 2 handfuls spinach
- 2 cups water
- 1½ cups frozen blueberries
- 1 banana, peeled
- 1 apple, cored and quartered
- 1 packet stevia
- 2 tablespoons ground flaxseeds
- OPTIONAL: 1 scoop of protein powder

Directions:

a) Place leafy greens and water into blender and blend until mixture is a green juice-like consistency.

b) Stop blender and add remaining ingredients. Blend until creamy.

4. Berry Peachy

Ingredients:

- 2 handfuls kale
- 1 handful spinach
- 2 cups water
- 2 apples, cored, quartered
- $1\frac{1}{2}$ cups frozen peaches
- $1\frac{1}{2}$ cups frozen mixed berries
- 2 packets stevia
- 2 tablespoons ground flaxseeds
- 1 scoop of protein powder

Directions:

a) Place leafy greens and water into blender and blend until mixture is a green juice-like consistency.

b) Stop blender and add remaining ingredients. Blend until creamy.

5. Peach Berry Spinach

Ingredients:

- 3 handfuls spinach

- 2 cups water

- 1 cup frozen peaches

- 1 handful fresh or frozen seedless grapes 1½ cups blueberries

- 3 packets stevia to sweeten

- 2 tablespoons ground flaxseeds

- OPTIONAL: 1 scoop of protein powder

Directions:

a) Place spinach and water into blender and blend until mixture is a green juice-like consistency. Stop blender and add remaining ingredients.

b) Blend until creamy.

6. Pineapple Spinach

Ingredients:

- 2 cups fresh spinach, packed
- 1 cup pineapple chunks
- 2 cups frozen peaches
- 2 bananas, peeled
- 1½ packets stevia
- 2 cups water
- 2 tablespoons ground flaxseeds
- OPTIONAL: 1 scoop of protein powder

Directions:

a) Place spinach and water into blender and blend until mixture is a green juice-like consistency. Stop blender and add remaining ingredients.

b) Blend until creamy.

7. Pineapple Berry

Ingredients:

- 2 handfuls spring mix greens
- 2 handfuls spinach
- 1 banana, peeled
- 1 $\frac{1}{2}$ cups pineapple chunks
- 1$\frac{1}{2}$ cups frozen mango chunks
- 1 cup frozen mixed berries
- 3 packets stevia
- 2 cups water
- 2 tablespoons ground flaxseeds
- OPTIONAL: 1 scoop of protein powder

Directions:

a) Place leafy greens and water into blender and blend until mixture is a green juice-like consistency. Stop blender and add remaining ingredients.

b) Blend until creamy.

8. Lingonberry smoothie

1 portion

Ingredients:

- 1-1½ cups (200-300 ml) water
- ½ cup (100 ml) almonds, soaked
- 2 apricots, soaked
- ¼ cup (50 ml) lingonberries, frozen or thawed

Directions:

a) Blend together 1 scant cup (200 ml) water with almonds to make a milk. Strain through a mesh sieve or a nut milk bag. Pour the strained milk into the blender. Add apricots and blend again.

b) Blend in the berries and add more water to desired consistency.

9. Spinach Kale Berry

Ingredients:

- 2 handfuls kale
- 2 handfuls spinach
- 2 cups water
- 1 apple, cored, quartered
- 1 banana, peeled
- 1½ cups frozen blueberries
- 2 packets stevia
- 2 tablespoons ground flaxseeds
- OPTIONAL: 1 scoop of protein powder

Directions:

a) Place leafy greens and water into blender and blend until mixture is a green juice-like consistency. Stop blender and add remaining ingredients.

b) Blend until creamy.

10. Apple Mango

Ingredients:

- 3 handfuls spinach
- 2 cups water
- 1 apple, cored, quartered
- $1\frac{1}{2}$ cups mangoes
- 2 cups frozen strawberries
- 1 packet stevia
- 2 tablespoons ground flaxseeds
- OPTIONAL: 1 scoop of protein powder

Directions:

a) Place spinach and water into blender and blend until mixture is a green juice-like consistency. Stop blender and add remaining ingredients to blender.

b) Blend until creamy.

11. Pineapple Kale

Ingredients:

- 2 handfuls kale

- 1 handful spring mix greens

- 2 cups water

- 1½ cups frozen peaches

- 2 handfuls pineapple chunks

- 2 packets stevia

- 2 tablespoons ground flaxseeds

- OPTIONAL: 1 scoop of protein powder

Directions:

a) Place leafy greens and water into blender and blend until mixture is a green juice-like consistency. Stop blender and add remaining ingredients.

b) Blend until creamy.

12. Daily Lime and Dill Detox

Serves: 2

Ingredients:

- 1/2 pear

- 1 cup chopped and seeded cucumber

- 1/4 cup chopped fresh dill

- 1 small avocado

- 1 cup baby spinach

- 2 tablespoons lime juice

- 1-inch knob fresh gingerroot, peeled

- 1 cup frozen pineapple

- 11/4 cups water

- 3 to 4 ice cubes

Directions:

a) Place all the ingredients except the ice in a Blender, and process until smooth and creamy.

b) Add the ice and process again. Drink chilled.

13. Peachy Kale Dream

Serves: 2

Ingredients:

- 1/2 avocado
- 1 cup frozen organic frozen peaches
- 1 frozen banana, cut into pieces
- 2 tablespoons fresh lemon juice
- 11/4 cups water
- handful of kale
- 3 to 4 ice cubes
- Optional: 2 to 3 pitted dates

Directions:

a) Place all the ingredients except the ice in a Blender, and process until smooth and creamy.

b) Add the ice and dates (if using) and process again. Drink chilled.

14. Watermelon Cooler

Serves: 2

Ingredients:

- 2 cups cubed seedless watermelon
- 1 whole cucumber, peeled, seeded, and coarsely chopped
- 1 large handful chopped kale
- 3 tablespoons fresh lime juice
- 1/4 cup chopped fresh mint
- 1/4 cup chopped fresh basil
- 1 cup ice cubes

Directions:

a) Place the watermelon and cucumber in a Blender, and process until smooth and creamy.

b) Add the remaining ingredients and process again. Drink ice cold.

15. Cinnamon Apple Smoothie

Serves: 1

Ingredients:

- 1 frozen banana, cut into bite-sized pieces

- 1 organic Granny Smith apple, cored and chopped (keep the skin on)

- 1 tablespoon fresh lemon juice

- 1 large handful baby spinach

- 1 cup cold water

- 2 to 3 pitted dates

- 1/2 teaspoon cinnamon

- 1/8 teaspoon nutmeg

- 4 to 5 ice cubes

Directions:

a) Place all the ingredients except the ice in a Blender, and process until smooth and creamy.

b) Add the ice and process again. Drink chilled.

16. Chocolaty Chia Smoothie

Serves: 2

Ingredients:

- 1 cup water

- 11/2 cups frozen organic strawberries

- 1 tablespoon chia seeds

- 2 tablespoons raw cacao nibs

- 1 tablespoon raw cacao powder

- 6 raw macadamia nuts

- 3 pitted dates

- 1 frozen banana, cut into bite-sized chunks

- 1 large handful chopped kale

- 4 to 5 ice cubes

Directions:

a) Put the water and strawberries in a Blender, and process until smooth and creamy.

b) Add the chia seeds, cacao nibs, cacao powder, and macadamia nuts; process for 1 full minute. Add the dates, frozen banana, and kale, and process again until well blended. Add the ice and process again.

c) Serve ice cold.

17. Green Tea and Ginger Smoothie

Serves: 2

Ingredients:

- 1 Anjou pear, chopped

- 1/4 cup white raisins or dried mulberries

- 1 teaspoon freshly minced gingerroot

- 1 large handful chopped romaine lettuce

- 1 tablespoon hemp seeds

- 1 cup unsweetened brewed green tea, cooled

- 7 to 9 ice cubes

Directions:

a) Place all the ingredients except the ice in a Blender, and process until smooth and creamy.

b) Add the ice and process again. Drink chilled.

18. Greeno-Colada

Serves: 1

Ingredients:

- 1 cup frozen chopped pineapple

- 3 tablespoons raw, unsweetened, shredded coconut

- 1 tablespoon fresh lime juice

- 1 handful baby spinach leaves

- 3 pitted dates

- 1 cup water

- 4 to 5 ice cubes

Directions:

a) Place all the ingredients except the ice in a Blender, and process until smooth and creamy. Add the ice and process again.

b) Drink ice cold.

19. Mint Chocolate Chip Smoothie

Serves: 2

Ingredients:

- 1 frozen banana, cut into bite-sized pieces

- 1/2 cup frozen peaches

- 1/2 cup raw macadamia nuts

- 1/3 cup chopped fresh mint leaves

- 3 tablespoons raw cacao nibs

- 2 to 3 pitted dates

- 1/2 teaspoon pure vanilla extract

- 11/2 cups water

- 3 or 4 ice cubes

Directions:

a) Place all the ingredients except the ice in a Blender, and process until smooth and creamy.

b) Add the ice and process again. Drink chilled.

20. Sunny C Delight No-Milk Shake

Serves: 1

Ingredients:

- 1 orange, peeled and chopped

- 1 kiwi, peeled and chopped

- 5 pitted dates

- 1/2 cup frozen pineapple

- 2 tablespoons hemp seeds

- 1/2 cup water

- 3 to 4 ice cubes

Directions:

a) Place all the ingredients except the ice in a Blender, and process until smooth and creamy.

b) Add the ice and process again. Drink chilled.

21. Strawberries and Cream

Serves: 1

Ingredients:

- 1/4 cup old-fashioned oats
- 3 tablespoons chopped raw macadamia nuts (preferably soaked for 1 to 2 hours)
- 1 cup frozen organic strawberries
- 4 pitted dates
- 1/4 teaspoon pure vanilla extract
- 1 cup ice-cold water
- 3 to 4 ice cubes

Directions:

a) Place all the ingredients except the ice in a Blender, and process until smooth and creamy.

b) Add the ice and process again. Drink chilled.

22. Lime No-Milk Shake

Serves: 2

Ingredients:

- 1 frozen banana, cut into bite-sized pieces

- 1/4 cup mashed avocado

- 2 tablespoons Nellie and Joe's Famous Key West Lime Juice

- 5 to 6 pitted dates

- 1/4 cup raw cashews

- 1/8 teaspoon pure vanilla extract

- 1/8 teaspoon unrefined sea salt

- 1 cup water

- 8 ice cubes

Directions:

a) Place all the ingredients except the ice in a Blender, and process until smooth and creamy.

b) Add the ice and process again. Drink chilled.

23. Ginger and Wild Blueberry

Serves: 2

Ingredients:

- 1 cup frozen wild blueberries (or regular cultivated frozen blueberries)

- 1/4 cup raw cashews

- 1 banana, cut into bite-sized pieces

- 1 tablespoon fresh lemon juice

- 1/2 teaspoon pure vanilla extract

- 1 tablespoon freshly grated gingerroot

- 5 to 6 pitted dates

- 1 cup cold water

- 5 to 6 ice cubes

Directions:

a) Place all the ingredients except the ice in a Blender, and process until smooth and creamy.

b) Add the ice and process again. Drink chilled.

24. Cappuccino No-Milk Shake

Serves: 1

Ingredients:

- 1 banana, cut into bite-sized pieces
- 1/2 cup water
- 2 tablespoons hemp seeds
- 8 almonds
- 1 teaspoon instant espresso powder
- 1/2 teaspoon cinnamon
- 1 teaspoon pure vanilla extract
- 4 prunes
- 11/2 cups ice

Directions:

a) Place all the ingredients except the ice in a Blender, and process until smooth and creamy.

b) Add the ice and process again. Drink ice cold.

25. Cherry Vanilla No-Milk Shake

Serves: 2

Ingredients:

- 1 cup frozen pitted cherries

- 1/4 cup raw macadamia nuts

- 1/2 banana, cut into chunks

- 1/4 cup dried goji berries (or white raisins)

- 1 teaspoon pure vanilla extract

- 1 cup water

- 6 to 8 ice cubes

Directions:

a) Place all the ingredients except the ice in a Blender, and process until smooth and creamy.

b) Add the ice and process again. Drink ice cold.

26.Goji and Chia Strawberry bowl

Total Time: 5 minutes

Yield: 1

Ingredients

- 1T goji berries
- 1T Strawberries
- 1-inch piece cinnamon stick
- 2-4T chia seeds
- 1 T coconut oil
- 16 oz. coconut water
- 2T cashew milk yogurt
- 1/3 c hemp seeds
- 2-3 large kale leaves
- 1c frozen berries
- $\frac{1}{2}$ frozen banana

Directions

a) Place goji berries, cinnamon, and chia seeds in your blender, and add enough coconut water to cover well. Let soak about 10 minutes.

b) Add the remaining coconut water and the rest of the ingredients to the blender and process on the appropriate setting for smoothies, adding extra liquid (coconut water, water, or nut milk) for your desired consistency.

27. Fruit and Coconut Milk Smoothie

Makes 4 servings

Ingredients

- 1 10-ounce bag frozen blueberries or other fruit
- 3 ripe bananas
- 1 cup plain yogurt
- 1 cup unsweetened coconut milk
- 2 tablespoons honey

Directions:

a) In a blender, puree the blueberries, bananas, yogurt, coconut milk, and honey.
b) Serve.

28. Slumbery Smoothie

Ingredients:

- 2 cups baby spinach
- 1 cup almond milk
- 1 banana, peeled and sliced
- 1 teaspoon honey

Directions:

a) Place all ingredients in a blender and puree.

29. Success Smoothie

Ingredients:

- 1 cup strawberries, sliced
- 1 cup blueberries
- ⅓ banana, sliced
- 1 teaspoon ground flaxseeds
- 1 handful spinach
- 1 teaspoon honey

Directions:

a) Blend everything together and enjoy!

30. Green smoothie with figs

1 serving

Ingredients:

- 2.5 ounces (70 g) baby spinach
- 1½-2 cups (300-500 ml) water
- 1 pear
- 2 figs, soaked

Directions:

a) Blend spinach with 1½ cups (300 ml) water. Cut the pear, add along with the figs, and blend again.

b) Add more water if needed to find the right consistency for your smoothie.

31. Kiwi breakfast

1 serving

Ingredients:

- 1 pear
- 2 celery stalks
- yellow kiwi fruits
- 1 tablespoon water
- $\frac{1}{2}$ teaspoon ground ginger

Directions:

a) Cut pears, celery, and one of the kiwis into large pieces and mix in the blender with 1 tablespoon water until it is a smooth consistency.

b) Top with the other kiwi, cut into pieces, and ground ginger.

32. Blackberries and fennel

Ingredients:

- 1 apple
- $\frac{1}{2}$ fennel
- $\frac{1}{4}$ cup (50 ml) water
- $\frac{1}{2}$ cup (100 ml) blackberries

Directions:

a) Cut the apple and fennel into pieces and mix with water in a blender.

b) Serve topped with blackberries.

33. Zucchini, Pear and Apple Bowl

1 serving

Ingredients:

- ½ zucchini

- 1 pear

- 1 apple

- optional: cinnamon and ground ginger

Directions:

a) Cut zucchini and pears into large chunks and blend in the food processor.

b) Add the apple, cut into large chunks, and continue blending to a smooth consistency.

c) Serve in a bowl and sprinkle with cinnamon and ginger.

34. Avocado and berries

Ingredients:

- 1 avocado

- 1 pear

- 3½ ounces (100 g) blueberries

Directions:

a) Cut the avocados and pears into pieces.

b) Mix together in a bowl and top with blueberries.

SUPER GREEN SMOOTHIES

35. Green Powerhouse

Ingredients:

- 1 Bunch Kale
- ½ Cucumber
- 4 Celery Stalks
- 1/3 Fennel Bulb and Stalk
- 1 Green Apple
- 1 Fuji Apple
- 1 Pear
- ½ Lemon
- 1 Inch Ginger

Directions:

a) Blend all ingredients to combine.

b) Enjoy.

36. Stomach Soother

Ingredients:

- 1 Small Head of Fennel
- 2 Stalks Celery
- 1 Handful of Mint
- 1 Bunch Flat Leaf Parsley
- ½ Green Apple
- 2 Small Lemons

Directions:

a) Blend all ingredients to combine.

b) Enjoy.

37. Immune Booster

Ingredients:

- $\frac{1}{2}$ Cucumber
- 2 Stalks Celery
- Handful of Spinach
- 1 Apple
- $\frac{1}{2}$ Lemon
- 1 Inch Ginger

Directions:

a) Blend all ingredients to combine.

b) Enjoy.

38. Ultra-cool Green Drink

Ingredients:

- 8 Kiwis
- 3 Green Apples
- 1/3 Cucumber
- 1 Piece of Fresh Ginger
- Handful of Fresh Mint

Directions:

a) Blend all ingredients to combine.

b) Enjoy.

39. Lungs Detox

Ingredients:

- 1 Cucumber
- 1 Head Romaine Lettuce
- 1 large Handful of Parsley
- 2 Meyer Lemons
- 1 Apple
- 1 Inch Ginger

Directions:

a) Blend all ingredients to combine.

b) Ginger is one of those ingredients that is centuries old and is both flavorful and powerful. It is a natural anti-inflammatory and has been shown to have dramatically impressive results in persons suffering from arthritis. Most importantly it is a powerful immune booster.

40. Zesty Afternoon Snack

Ingredients:

- 3 Apples
- 1 Cucumber
- 1 Lemon
- 5 Kale Stalks

Directions:

a) Blend all ingredients to combine.

b) Enjoy.

41. Spinach with Pineapple

Ingredients:

- ½ Pineapple
- 1 Cucumber
- 2 Bunches of Spinach

Directions:

a) Blend all ingredients to combine.

b) Enjoy.

42. Metabolism Booster

Ingredients:

- 1 Cucumber
- 3 Stalks Celery
- Handful of Fresh Mint
- 2 Kale Leaves
- 1 Peeled Lemon

Directions:

a) Blend all ingredients to combine.

b) Enjoy.

43. Ultra-green Wake Up

Ingredients:

- 1 Pear
- 1 Cucumber
- 4 Stalks Celery
- 3 Sprigs Mint
- 4 Small Limes

Directions:

a) Blend all ingredients to combine.

b) Enjoy.

44. Afternoon Cooler

Ingredients:

- 1 Apple
- 1 Pear
- $\frac{1}{2}$ Cucumber
- 3 Kale Leaves
- Handful Fresh Mint

Directions:

a) Blend all ingredients to combine.

b) Enjoy.

45. Stimulating Smoothie

Ingredients:

- 1 Bunch Kale
- Large Handful of Fresh Mint
- 2 Apples
- 1 Lemon Peeled

Directions:

a) Blend all ingredients to combine.

b) Enjoy.

46. Citrus Delight

Ingredients:

- 4 Cups Spinach
- 1 Bunch Kale
- 2 Oranges
- 1 Cucumber

Directions:

a) Blend all ingredients to combine.

b) Enjoy.

HIGH PROTEIN GREEN SMOOTHIES

47. Cashew Blast

Ingredients:

- 5-7 Kernels of Cashew Nuts
- Spinach Leaves
- Lemon Syrup
- Curd
- Sugar

Directions

a) Half boil the spinach leaves and get rid of its raw appeal. Mix the lemon syrup and thick curd thoroughly in a bowl. Grind cashew kernels and sugar to give a coarse mixture.

b) Put the half-boiled leaves into the curd and add the coarse cashew kernels with sugar. Finally blend a little to give a uniform texture. Enjoy this smoothie with bread toasts.

48. Yogurt with Cinnamon

Ingredients:

- 1 Ripe Cucumber
- 1 cup Oat Milk
- A pinch of Cinnamon
- Salt
- Coriander Leaves
- Probiotic yogurt

Directions

a) Chop the cucumber into medium sized pieces and blend all ingredients except cinnamon in a grinder. Put it into the refrigerator for a while.

a) Just before serving, add a pinch of cinnamon and garnish with coriander leaves.

49. Peanuts with Mint and Honey

Ingredients:

- Peanuts without shells
- 1 handful Mint Leaves
- Thick curd
- Honey
- Ice cubes

Directions

a) Grind all ingredients together to form a thick uniform paste.

b) Lastly, add the ice cubes and serve cold.

50. Kiwi Guava Burst

Ingredients:

- 1 Kiwi
- 1 Guava
- Coconut Water
- Fresh Corn Kernels
- Ice Cubes

Directions

a) Chop the kiwi and guava into small pieces.

b) Grind the corn kernels with coconut water and add the chopped fruit pieces into it. Serve with ice cubes.

51. Spinach Surprise

Ingredients:

- Bread Slices
- Spinach Leaves
- Yogurt
- Lemon Syrup

Directions

a) Blend the spinach leaves in yogurt. Add bread slices and blend again to get a thick texture.

b) Add lemon syrup to taste and serve at room temperature.

52. Lychee with Eggs and Honey

Ingredients:

- Egg whites
- Milk
- 7-8 lychees
- 2 cucumbers
- Honey

Directions

a) Blend the egg white thoroughly with milk and honey. Peel and chop lychees into small pieces and keep aside. Blend the cucumbers with the milk mixture. Add the lychee pieces such that they float in the smoothie.

b) This will give flavor and taste like none other.

53. Almond and Banana

Ingredients:

- 1 Medium Banana
- Cubed Pineapple Pieces
- Fresh Mint Leaves
- Roasted Almonds
- Ice Cubes

Directions

a) Slice the almonds into fine pieces and keep aside. Blend the banana, pineapple and mint leaves together with ice cubes to give slush like mixture.

b) Garnish with slices almonds just before serving.

54. Lettuce with Yogurt and Orange

Ingredients:

- Organic Lettuce Leaves
- Fresh Thick Yogurt
- Orange Pulp
- Ice

Directions

a) Blend the yogurt with orange pulp to give a smooth pulpy texture. Half boil the lettuce and add the chopped leaves into the yogurt mixture.

b) Blend thoroughly. Finally, add crushed ice to this mixture and serve chilled.

55. Pear and Banana Blast

Ingredients:

- 1 Organic Pear
- Coriander Stalks
- Milk
- 1 Ripe Banana
- Sugar

Directions

a) Chop the pear into smaller pieces and keep aside. Crush the coriander stalks in milk. Add the ripe banana to milk and blend well. Add sugar to taste and add the chopped pear pieces to the smoothie.

b) As an option, you can add mint leaves into the smoothie to enhance the taste and flavor.

56. Spirulina Smoothie

Ingredients:

- 1 Teaspoon Spirulina
- 2-3 centimeter Knob of Ginger
- Spinach Leaves
- Fruit yogurt
- Hot water

Directions

a) Blend the spirulina with the spinach leaves together to give a thick paste. Dilute the paste with fruit yogurt according to taste and preferred texture.

b) Boil the ginger in hot water and extract its flavor. Add the ginger extract to the mixture of spinach and spirulina.

c) Heat the mixture till it turns lukewarm and drink the smoothie in that temperature, preferably before meals.

57. Fig and Walnut Smoothie

Ingredients:

- 1-2 Fresh Figs
- 3 Strawberries
- Salt
- Walnuts
- Coriander Leaves
- Ice Cubes
- Milk

Directions

a) Add milk, strawberries, figs and coriander leaves to the milk and blend it until it turns smooth and even.

b) Break the walnuts into smaller pieces and crush it with the required amount of salt.

c) Add the coarse walnut crush just before you serve. Serve chilled.

58. Pistachios and Banana Smoothie

Ingredients:

- Pistachios
- Warm Water
- 1 Apple
- 1 Banana
- 3 Cucumbers

Directions

a) Add chopped apple pieces into warm water and crush the banana into a paste. Grate the cucumbers and add them to the banana paste.

b) Mix the paste well and add it to the warm water containing apple pieces. Do not blend. Chop the pistachios into two and add them to the apple pulp. Now mix just the banana paste and apple pulp.

c) Use the warm water to even out the texture. Serve warm.

59. Soy Smoothie

Ingredients:

- Egg Whites
- Soy Milk
- Cottage Cheese
- Sugar
- Salt

Directions

a) Blend the egg whites, soy milk and cottage cheese to give a grainy texture to the smoothie. Add sugar and salt in a proportion that adds flavor to the tongue.

b) On the smoothie, again grate some cottage cheese.

60. Cow Pea Smoothie

Ingredients:

- Thick Yogurt
- Orange Pulp
- Cow Peas
- Mint Leaves
- Fresh Onions
- Protein Source: Egg Whites, Soy Milk, Cottage Cheese.

Directions

a) Finely chop the onions and sauté them over a low flame. Put them aside. Half boil the cow peas so as to make them spongy and soft.

b) Blend the yogurt, orange pulp and onions together to make a thick paste. Add the cow peas in the end.

c) Use mint leaves to garnish it while serving. Serve chilled.

DETOX SMOOTHIES FOR BREAKFAST

61. Green Detox Machine

Ingredients:

- 1/2 cup Orange Juice
- 2 teaspoons Ginger
- 2 cups Kale
- 1/2 cup Cilantro
- 1 Lime (remove the seeds, keep the peel)
- 1 Green Apple
- 1 Banana (frozen, chopped)

Directions:

a) Blend all ingredients to combine.

b) Enjoy.

62. Green Leafy Smoothie

Ingredients:

- 1/2 cup Apple Juice
- 2 cups Mixed Greens
- 1 cup Spinach
- 1 Lemon (remove the seeds, keep the peel)
- 1 Pear
- 1 Banana (frozen, chopped)

Directions:

a) Blend all ingredients to combine.

b) Enjoy.

63. Green Avocado Smoothie

Ingredients:

- 3/4 cup Coconut Water
- 1/2 cup Kale
- 1/2 cup Spinach
- 1/2 cup Avocado
- 2 cups Seedless Grapes
- 1 Pear
- 4 - 5 Ice Cubes

Directions:

a) Blend all ingredients to combine.

b) Enjoy.

64. Carrot Smoothie

Ingredients:

- 1/2 cup Water
- 1/2 cup Skim Milk
- 1/2 tsp. Cinnamon
- 1/8 cup Old-Fashioned Rolled Oats
- 1/2 cup Spinach
- 2 Small Carrots or 1 Large Carrot (with green tops)
- 1 Banana (frozen, chopped)
- 4 - 5 Ice Cubes

Directions:

a) Blend all ingredients to combine.

b) Enjoy.

65. Green Melon Smoothie

Ingredients:

- 1/2 cup Water
- 3 tbsp. Honey
- 1 Lime Wedge (remove the seeds, keep the peel)
- 1 cup Kale
- 1/2 cup Cantaloupe
- 1/2 cup Honeydew
- 4 - 5 Ice Cubes

Directions:

a) Blend all ingredients to combine.

b) Enjoy.

66. Refreshing Cucumber Delight

Ingredients:

- 1/2 cup Water
- 4 tbsp. Honey
- 2 cups Kale
- 1 Lime Wedge (remove the seeds, keep the peel)
- 2 Cucumbers (remove seeds and peel)
- 4 - 5 Ice Cubes

Directions:

a) Blend all ingredients to combine.

b) Enjoy.

67. Berry Green Smoothie

Ingredients:

- 1/2 cup Apple Juice
- 1 cup Spinach
- 2 cups Mixed Berries
- 1 Banana (frozen, chopped)
- 4 - 5 Ice Cubes

Directions:

a) Blend all ingredients to combine.

b) Enjoy.

68. Banana Smoothie

Ingredients:

- 1/2 cup Milk
- 1/2 cup Vanilla Yogurt
- 2 tsp. Honey
- 1/4 tsp. Cinnamon
- 2 Bananas
- 1 cup Spinach
- 4 - 5 Ice Cubes

Directions:

a) Blend all ingredients to combine.

b) Enjoy.

69. Watermelon Smoothie

Ingredients:

- 2 cups Watermelon
- 1 cup Spinach
- 1/2 cup Strawberries
- 1/2 cup Frozen Peaches
- 4 - 5 Ice Cubes

Directions:

a) Blend all ingredients to combine.

b) Enjoy.

70. Peanut Butter Smoothie

Ingredients:

- 1 cup Skim Milk
- 3 tbsp. Peanut Butter
- 2 cups Spinach
- 1 Banana (frozen, chopped)

Directions:

a) Blend all ingredients to combine.

b) Enjoy.

71. Strawberry Banana Smoothie

Ingredients:

- 1/2 cup Water
- 1/2 cup Skim Milk
- 1/2 cup Vanilla Yogurt
- 2 tsp. Honey
- 1 cup Mixed Greens
- 1/2 cup Strawberries
- 1 Banana (frozen, chopped)
- 4 - 5 Ice Cubes

Directions:

a) Blend all ingredients to combine.

b) Enjoy.

72. Almond Dream

Ingredients:

- 1 cup Almond Milk
- 3 tbs. Almond Butter
- 1 cup Kale
- 1 cup Spinach
- 1/4 cup Blueberries
- 1/4 cup Blackberries
- 4 -5 Ice Cubes

Directions:

a) Blend all ingredients to combine.

b) Enjoy.

73. Green Fruit and Nut Smoothie

Ingredients:

- 1 cup Almond Milk
- 1/4 cup Sunflower Seeds
- 1/4 cup Cashews
- 3 cups Spinach
- 2 Dates
- 1/2 cup Blueberries
- 1 Banana
- 4 - 5 Ice Cubes

Directions:

a) Blend all ingredients to combine.

b) Enjoy.

74. Minty Green Smoothie

Ingredients:

- 1/2 cup Apple Juice
- 1 tbsp. Ground Ginger
- 1/4 cup Mint Leaves
- 1 cup Spinach
- 1cup Kale
- 1 Pear
- 4 - 5 Ice Cubes

Directions:

a) Blend all ingredients to combine.

b) Enjoy.

DETOX SMOOTHIES FOR LUNCH

75. Celery Green Smoothie

Ingredients:

- 1 stalk Celery, sliced thin
- 4 Real Ripe Bananas
- A handful of Baby Spinach
- 1 cup Ice Water or Ice Cubes

Directions:

a) Add all these ingredients to the blender and puree until smooth.

76. Collard Green smoothie

Ingredients:

- 4 oz. Coconut Water
- 1 Frozen Banana
- 1 cup Blueberries
- 1 cup Seedless Grapes
- A handful of Collard Greens, without the stems and stalk.
- $\frac{1}{2}$ cup Ice Water or Ice Cubes

Directions:

a) Add all these ingredients to the blender and puree until it is a smoothie. This one is really good.

b) All that mixture of flavors would make a tasty lunch.

77. Mango Green Smoothie

Ingredients:

- 1 Frozen Banana
- 1 Mango, sliced
- 2 good handfuls of Baby Spinach
- 1cup Ice Water

Directions:

a) Add all these ingredients to the blender and puree until smooth

78. Spicy Delicious Green Smoothie

Ingredients:

- ½ cup of Pure Vanilla Almond Milk
- 1 Banana
- Dash of Cinnamon
- 1 handful of Spinach
- 1 tablespoon Whey Powder
- 1 cup Ice

Directions:

a) Add all these ingredients to the blender and puree until smooth.

79. All Purpose Green Smoothie

Ingredients:

- 1 Banana
- 1 sliced Apple
- 1 sliced Pear
- 1 stalk Celery, cut up
- $\frac{1}{2}$ Lemon
- 2 handfuls of Spinach
- 1 handful Romaine Lettuce
- Little bit of Parsley
- Little bit of Cilantro
- 1 cup Ice

Directions:

a) Add all the ingredients to the blender then squeeze the lemon over it. Puree until it is smooth.

80. Green Tea Smoothie

Ingredients:

- 1 cup Green Tea
- 1 Carrot
- 1 Banana
- 2 handfuls Kale (with the no stems or stalk)
- Few Ice Cubes

Directions:

a) Add all the ingredients to the blender and puree until smooth. This one is a great choice for lunch.

81. Lemon Cucumber Green Smoothie

Ingredients:

- 1 Cucumber
- 1 Pear, sliced
- 4 Celery Stalks
- 1 peeled Lemon
- $\frac{1}{2}$ cup Ice Water

Directions:

a) Add all these ingredients to the blender and puree until they are smooth.

b) Perfect selection for lunch; this one will give you the energy you need for the rest of the afternoon.

82. Cashew Green Smoothie

Ingredients:

- 1 cup Coconut Water
- ½ cup Cashews
- 1 Banana
- 2 Dates
- 1 tablespoons Flax Seed
- One handful of Spinach

Directions:

a) Add all the ingredients to the blender and puree until it is smooth.

b) This one is delicious and the cashews give it something special. Great choice for lunch

83. Orange Green Smoothie

Ingredients:

- 1 Banana
- 5 Large Strawberries
- $\frac{1}{2}$ cup Peeled Orange
- $\frac{1}{2}$ cup sliced Apple
- Little bit of Flax Seed
- 2 handfuls of Spinach
- 1 cup Ice Water

Directions:

a) Mix all the ingredients into the blender and puree until smooth.

b) This one is wonderful and perfect for lunch.

84. Fruit and Green Smoothie

Ingredients:

- 1 small container Plain Greek Yogurt
- 1/2cup Natural Protein Powder
- $\frac{1}{2}$ cup Blueberries
- $\frac{1}{2}$ cup Peaches, sliced
- $\frac{1}{2}$ cup Pineapple, sliced
- $\frac{1}{2}$ cup Strawberries
- $\frac{1}{2}$ cup Mango, sliced
- 1 handful of Kale (remove stem and stalks)
- $\frac{1}{2}$ cup Ice Water

Directions:

a) Add all these ingredients to the blender and puree until smooth.

b) This one is out of this world.

85. Ginger Green Smoothie

Ingredients:

- Small handful of parsley
- 1 Cucumber, sliced
- 1 peeled Lemon
- 1 inch of Ginger Root
- 1 cup Frozen Apples
- 1 handful Kale (without the stems and stalks)
- $\frac{1}{2}$ cup Ice Water

Directions:

a) Mix all these ingredients into the blender and puree until smooth. This one is very good.

b) All these ingredients are wonderful together. Good choice for lunch

86. Melon Green Shake

Ingredients:

- ½ cup Black Cherries, pitted
- 1 Banana
- Little handful of Kale, cut up
- ½ cup Blueberries
- ½ cup Green Melon
- ½ cup Coconut Water
- ½ cup Ice Cubes

Directions:

a) Add all these ingredients to the blender and puree until it is smooth. This one is very good.

b) All the flavors are wonderful together.

87. Almond Coconut Yogurt Green Smoothie

Ingredients:

- 1 cup Almond Coconut Yogurt
- Bunch of Cilantro
- Handful of Spinach
- Avocado, sliced
- 1 cup Blueberries, Strawberries or Raspberries
- 1 Mango, sliced
- $\frac{1}{2}$ cup Coconut Water
- Pinch of Sea Salt
- Ice Water

Directions:

a) Add all the ingredients to the blender and puree until smooth. Add the water as needed. This is a delicious green smoothie with a great taste.

b) All this mixture of flavors is a treat to drink.

88. Refreshing Green Smoothie

Ingredients:

- 1 cup Pineapple, cut up
- 1 Frozen Banana, cut up
- 1 Mango, sliced
- $\frac{1}{2}$ cup Ice Water
- Handful Baby Spinach

Directions:

a) Add all the ingredients to the blender and puree until smooth. This one is really delicious and refreshing.

b) This is a great choice for lunch.

DETOX SMOOTHIES FOR DINNER

89. Minty Raspberry Green Smoothie

MAKES: 2 servings

Ingredients:

- $1\frac{1}{2}$ cups (78g) Dandelion Greens
- $\frac{1}{4}$ cup (23g) chopped Mint
- $2\frac{1}{2}$ cups (308g) frozen Raspberries
- 1 pitted Medjool Date
- 2 tablespoons ground Flaxseeds
- Purified Water

Directions:

a) Add all the ingredients except the purified water to the tall cup. Add water as desired while ensuring that it doesn't pass the Max Line.

b) Process until smooth.

90. Berry Cleanser Smoothie

MAKES: 2 servings

Ingredients:

- 3 Swiss Chard leaves, stems removed
- $\frac{1}{4}$ cup (28g) ripe Cranberries
- 2 cups (288g) Blueberries
- 1 pitted Medjool Date
- 2 tablespoons ground Flaxseeds
- Purified Water

Directions:

a) Add all the ingredients except the purified water to the tall cup. Add water as desired while ensuring that it doesn't pass the Max Line.

b) Process until smooth.

91. Green Twist Smoothie

MAKES: 2 servings

Ingredients:

- 1 cup (67g) Kale, stems removed, ribs removed and chopped

- 1 cup (55g) Dandelion Greens

- 1 Orange, peeled, seeded and chopped

- 2 cups (288g) Strawberries

- 2 Kiwis, peeled and chopped

- $\frac{1}{2}$ tablespoon Lemon juice

- Purified Water

Directions:

a) Add all the ingredients except the purified water to the tall cup. Add water as desired while ensuring that it doesn't pass the Max Line.

b) Process until smooth.

92. Pina Colada Green Smoothie

MAKES: 2 servings

Ingredients:

- 2 cups (76g) Beet Greens
- 1 cup (166g) fresh Pineapple, chopped
- 1 cup (144g) Blueberries
- 1 tablespoon ground Flaxseeds
- 1 tablespoon organic Coconut Oil
- 1 cup (240ml) Coconut Water
- Purified Water

Directions:

a) Add all the ingredients except the purified water to the tall cup. Add water as desired while ensuring that it doesn't pass the Max Line.

b) Process until smooth.

93. Watercress Cranberry Cooler

MAKES: 2 servings

Ingredients:

- 2 cups (70g) Watercress
- $\frac{1}{4}$ cup (28g) fresh ripe Cranberries
- 1 ripe Banana, sliced
- 1 Orange, peeled and chopped
- 1 pitted Medjool Date (optional)
- 1 tablespoon powdered Wheatgrass
- Purified Water

Directions:

a) Add all the ingredients except the purified water to the tall cup. Add water as desired while ensuring that it doesn't pass the Max Line.

b) Process until smooth.

94. Grape Berry Smoothie

MAKES: 2 servings

Ingredients:

- 2 cups (60g) fresh Baby Spinach, stems removed and chopped

- $\frac{1}{2}$ cup (46g) seedless Green Grapes

- 1 cup (124g) Raspberries

- 1 Medjool Date (optional)

- 2 tablespoons Chia seeds

- 1 teaspoon organic Cinnamon powder

- Purified Water

Directions:

a) Add all the ingredients except the purified water to the tall cup. Add water as desired while ensuring that it doesn't pass the Max Line.

b) Process until smooth.

95. Blueberry Ginger Green Smoothie

MAKES: 2 servings

Ingredients:

- 2 cups (60g) Baby Spinach

- 2 cups (288g) Blueberries

- 1 ripe Banana, sliced

- 1-inch (2cm) Ginger Root, washed and chopped

- 2 cups (480ml) organic Coconut Water

- Purified Water (optional)

Directions:

a) Add all the ingredients except the purified water to the tall cup. Add water as desired while ensuring that it doesn't pass the Max Line.

b) Process until smooth.

96. Avocado Apple Green Smoothie

MAKES: 2 servings

Ingredients:

- 2 cups (76g) Spring Greens
- 1 green Apple, cored and chopped
- 1 slice (100g) Avocado
- $\frac{1}{2}$ cup (46g) red Grapes
- $\frac{1}{2}$ cup (77g) Blueberries
- $\frac{1}{2}$ teaspoon Lemon juice
- Purified Water

Directions:

a) Add all the ingredients except the purified water to the tall cup. Add water as desired while ensuring that it doesn't pass the Max Line.

b) Process until smooth.

97. Sleek Swiss Chia

MAKES: 2 servings

Ingredients:

- ½ cup (30g) fresh Parsley
- 1½ cups (54g) Swiss Chard, chopped
- 2 ripe Peaches, pitted and chopped
- 1 Medjool date
- 1 cup (144g) Strawberries
- 2 tablespoons Chia seeds
- Purified Water

Directions:

a) Add all the ingredients except the purified water to the tall cup. Add water as desired while ensuring that it doesn't pass the Max Line.

b) Process until smooth.

98. Spring Green Power Smoothie

MAKES: 2 servings

Ingredients:

- 2 cups (76g) Spring Greens

- 1 ripe Mango, cubed

- 1 Orange, peeled, seeded and chopped

- 1 cup (124g) Raspberries

- 2 tablespoons Chia seeds

- 1 tablespoon ground Flaxseeds

- Purified Water

Directions:

a) Add all the ingredients except the purified water to the tall cup. Add water as desired while ensuring that it doesn't pass the Max Line.

b) Process until smooth.

99. Green Coco Berry Smoothie

MAKES: 2 servings

Ingredients:

- 2 cups (72g) Swiss Chard, torn
- ½ cup (83g) Pineapple chunks, sliced
- 1 cup (144g) Blueberries
- 1 cup (152g) Honeydew Melon, chopped
- 1 tablespoon extra-virgin Coconut Oil
- Purified Water

Directions:

a) Add all the ingredients except the purified water to the tall cup. Add water as desired while ensuring that it doesn't pass the Max Line.

b) Process until smooth.

100. Mixed Goji Berries Smoothie

MAKES: 2 servings

Ingredients:

- 2 cups (110g) Romaine Lettuce, chopped

- 1 ripe Banana, sliced

- $\frac{1}{4}$ cup (30g) Goji Berries

- 1 cup (144g) mixed Berries

- 1-inch (2.5cm) Ginger Root

- Purified Water

Directions:

a) Add all the ingredients except the purified water to the tall cup. Add water as desired while ensuring that it doesn't pass the Max Line.

b) Process until smooth.

CONCLUSION

Starting your morning with a green smoothie can help set a great tone for the entire day. Most of these detox smoothies are only 100 calories per serving so you'll want to pair it with something else, like an egg or some peanut butter on whole-wheat toast, if it's going to be a meal. You can also enjoy it as a snack. The smoothies are loaded with antioxidant-rich superfoods, and they are naturally sweet to crush your sugar cravings with no added sugar.

CPSIA information can be obtained
at www.ICGtesting.com
Printed in the USA
LVHW082018270222
712156LV00002B/44